Microwave
COOKING FOR 1&2

Text by Judith Ferguson
Photography by Peter Barry
Designed by Philip Clucas
CLB 1682
© 1987 Illustrations and text: Colour Library Books Ltd.,
   Guildford, Surrey, England.
Text filmsetting by Focus Photoset Ltd., London, England.
Printed and bound in Barcelona, Spain by Cronion, S.A.
All rights reserved.
1987 edition published by Crescent Books
   distributed by Crown Publishers, Inc.
ISBN 0 517 62736 1
h g f e d c b a

Microwave
COOKING FOR 1&2

CRESCENT BOOKS
NEW YORK

CONTENTS

INTRODUCTION

Do meals for singles or couples have to be uninspiring? Do people on their own have to rely on pre-prepared food for speed and convenience? Not when there is a microwave around. Small portions cook beautifully in practically the time it takes to open the package and read the cooking instructions. With a microwave oven there is no need to sacrifice variety for convenience.

Small packages of fresh vegetables and meat are readily available in supermarkets and specialty food stores. Even turkey and duck are available in manageable sizes for the small household. Cooking a dinner party for one special guest can be cheaper than dinner out. It can also be an occasion for experimenting with more elaborate preparations than you might want to attempt for large numbers.

However, leftovers come in handy, so don't shy away from cooking a whole turkey or a large piece of meat. Leftovers can be frozen and used as a basis for completely different meals later on. Small portions, well covered, will defrost in 2-3 minutes on a LOW or DEFROST setting. Soups can be kept refrigerated for up to two days and reheated on MEDIUM in about 2-5 minutes. Vegetable and flour-thickened soups can also be frozen, and then defrosted and reheated in about 10 minutes on a LOW or DEFROST setting, with frequent stirring. Meat, poultry and game stews and braises can be reheated as well, usually on MEDIUM for about 4-6 minutes. If frozen, they can be defrosted and reheated in about 12-15 minutes on LOW or DEFROST. Individual portions should be frozen in bags or containers that are suitable for reheating in microwave ovens or in individual serving dishes of the freezer-to-table variety.

All the recipes in this book were tested in an oven with a maximum power of 700 watts. Certain recipes were cooked in a combination microwave-convection oven, which combines the speed of microwave cooking with browning ability. However, any dish that requires browning can be placed under a preheated broiler for a minute or two before serving. Also, toppings such as breadcrumbs, crushed cereals or cheeses can give an eye-pleasing finish to your very own brand of 'convenience' food.

Microwave
COOKING FOR 1 & 2

SOUPS AND APPETIZERS

Confetti Spread and Sesame Crackers

PREPARATION TIME: 15 minutes

MICROWAVE COOKING TIME:
10-12 minutes

SERVES: 2 people

SPREAD
1 cup cream cheese
2 strips bacon, diced
1 tbsp chopped chives
Red pepper flakes
4 chopped black olives
Crushed garlic
¼ cup chopped green and red peppers,
  mixed
2 tbsps frozen corn
Salt and pepper

CRACKERS
¼ cup all-purpose flour
¼ cup whole-wheat flour
1½ tbsps butter
2 tsps sesame seeds
1-2 tbsps cold water
1 egg, beaten with a pinch of salt
Salt and pepper

Put the flours, salt and pepper into the bowl of a food processor. Cut the butter into small pieces and add to the flour. Process until the mixture looks like fine breadcrumbs. Add 1 tbsp sesame seeds and add the water with the machine running until the mixture forms a dough. Roll out thinly on a floured board and brush with the egg. Sprinkle on the remaining sesame seeds and cut into 1″ squares. Arrange into a circle on a large plate and cook on HIGH for 3-6 minutes until crisp. Cool on a wire rack. Makes 12 crackers.
Heat a browning dish for 3 minutes and cook the diced bacon on HIGH for 1-2 minutes or until crisp. Drain on paper towels and allow to cool. Put the chopped peppers and corn into a small bowl and cover with water. Cover the bowl with pierced plastic wrap and cook on HIGH for 2 minutes. Rinse with cold water and leave to drain dry. Put the cream

This page: Confetti Spread with Sesame Crackers. Facing page: Oriental Kebabs.

cheese into a small bowl and heat for 30-40 seconds on MEDIUM to soften. Add the bacon, peppers and the remaining ingredients, and mix

well. Serve with the sesame seed crackers. Unused peppers can be frozen.

Marinated Shrimp and Sour Cream Sauce

PREPARATION TIME: 15 minutes

MICROWAVE COOKING TIME: 5 minutes

SERVES: 2 people

½ lb fresh large shrimp, shelled and cleaned

MARINADE
½ cup white wine
2 tbsps white wine vinegar
1 bay leaf
2 black peppercorns
1 whole allspice berry
2 whole cloves
½ tsp dill seeds
½ small onion, sliced
Salt

SAUCE
½ cup sour cream
2-3 tbsps strained reserved marinade
½ tsp chopped dill, fresh or dried
½ tsp grated horseradish
Salt and pepper

GARNISH
Lettuce leaves
Sprigs of fresh dill

Combine all the marinade ingredients in a 1 pint casserole and cover. Cook for 2-3 minutes on HIGH until boiling. Stir in the shrimp, cover, and cook on MEDIUM for 2 minutes. Allow to cool in the marinade. If using fresh dill, reserve 2 small sprigs for garnish and chop ½ tsp. Drain the marinade and mix with the sour cream, dill, horseradish, and salt and pepper. Arrange lettuce on serving plates, and place on the shrimp. Top with some of the sauce and the reserved dill. Serve remaining sauce separately.

Scallop Parcels with Curry Sauce

PREPARATION TIME: 15 minutes

MICROWAVE COOKING TIME: 3-4 minutes

SERVES: 2 people

6 large or 8 small scallops
1 small sweet red pepper
2 large mushrooms
2 tbsps white wine
1 tsp black pepper
¼ tsp salt
¼ tsp ground ginger
Garlic powder
1 tbsp oil
Whole fresh chives

SAUCE
1 tbsp curry powder
½ cup plain yogurt
Juice of ½ a lime
½ tsp mango chutney
Salt and pepper

Mix the wine, salt, pepper, oil, ginger, and a pinch of garlic powder together well. Put in the scallops and turn them to coat evenly. Cut the pepper into pieces the size of the scallops. Cut the mushrooms into ¼" slices. Layer the pepper, mushrooms and scallops, and tie each parcel with 2 whole chives. Put the parcels on their sides onto a microwave roasting rack and cook on HIGH for 30 seconds. Turn every 30 seconds, ending with the parcels scallop-sides up. Cook for a total of 2-3 minutes, brushing frequently with the ginger basting liquid. Serve hot or cold, with the curry sauce.
Put the curry powder for the sauce onto a small plate and cook for 1 minute on HIGH. Allow to cool, and combine with the other ingredients. Serve with the scallops.

Oriental Kebabs

PREPARATION TIME: 20 minutes

MICROWAVE COOKING TIME: 5-6 minutes

SERVES: 2 people

3oz ground pork or beef
1 tbsp breadcrumbs
1 tsp chopped onion
1 small can pineapple chunks
6 cherry tomatoes

BASTING MIXTURE
¼ cup honey
¼ cup soy sauce
¼ cup rice wine
1 tbsp sesame seed oil
1 tsp ground ginger
Pepper

SWEET AND SOUR SAUCE
Remaining basting mixture
1 tbsp ketchup
1 tsp cornstarch
Reserved pineapple juice
1 tbsp cider vinegar
½ tsp garlic powder

Mix together the basting ingredients. Mix the meat, breadcrumbs, chopped onion and 1 tbsp of the basting mixture. Shape into 8 meatballs. Drain the can of pineapple and reserve the juice. Thread the meatballs onto wooden skewers, alternating with the pineapple chunks and tomatoes. Place the kebabs on a roasting rack and brush with the baste. Cook on HIGH for 3 minutes, turning and basting each minute. Combine the ingredients for the sauce, and cook on HIGH for 2-3 minutes until thickened. Stir every 30 seconds. Serve with the kebabs. For one person only, use half the amount of all the ingredients. Cook the kebabs for 2 minutes, and the sauce for 1-2 minutes.

Tomato and Basil Soup

PREPARATION TIME: 15 minutes

MICROWAVE COOKING TIME: 5 minutes

SERVES: 2 people

Facing page: Scallop Parcels with Curry Sauce (top) and Marinated Shrimp and Sour Cream Sauce (bottom).

vegetables lengthwise into thin strips. Add the carrot noodles to the consommé, cover with pierced plastic wrap, and cook on HIGH for 3 minutes. Add the zucchini and cook for an additional 1 minute on HIGH. Stir in the sherry before serving.

Cheesy Spinach Soup

PREPARATION TIME: 15 minutes

MICROWAVE COOKING TIME: 5 minutes

SERVES: 1 person

½ cup frozen spinach
½ cup shredded Colby cheese
2 tbsps hot water
1 tbsp butter
1 tbsp flour
½ a chicken bouillon cube
1 tbsp chopped onion
1 cup milk
Pinch of thyme
Pinch of nutmeg
Salt and pepper

2 cups tomato sauce
1 cup hot water
½ a beef bouillon cube, or 1 tsp instant
    beef bouillon granules
2 tbsps cream
2 tbsps red wine
¼ tsp cornstarch
Pinch sugar
2 tbsps fresh basil leaves
2 tbsps parsley
½ clove garlic
2 tbsps olive oil
Salt and pepper

Mix the tomato sauce, water, beef bouillon, sugar, and salt and pepper together in a 1 quart casserole. Cover and cook for 2 minutes on HIGH. Mix the cornstarch and wine together and stir into the soup. Heat for 2 minutes on HIGH, stirring every 30 seconds. Put the basil leaves, parsley and garlic into a blender and purée. Add the oil in a thin, steady stream with the machine running. Re-heat the soup for 1 minute on HIGH, and stir in the cream just before serving. Add the basil mixture, and stir through the

soup.
To serve one person only, use half of all the ingredients, and cook the soup for a total of 2 minutes.

Consommé with Vegetable Noodles

PREPARATION TIME: 15 minutes

MICROWAVE COOKING TIME: 5 minutes

SERVES: 2 people

10½ oz can condensed beef or chicken
    consommé
1½ cups water
1 bay leaf
1 tbsp sherry
1 small zucchini
1 small carrot, peeled

Combine the consommé and the water. Add the bay leaf and heat through for 1 minute on HIGH. Cut ends off the zucchini and carrot and, using a swivel peeler, pare the

Put the spinach, onion and water into a small bowl and cover with pierced plastic wrap. Cook for 1 minute on HIGH and set aside. Put the butter into another bowl and cook for 30 seconds on HIGH or until melted. Add the flour, bouillon cube, nutmeg, thyme, milk, and salt and pepper. Cook on MEDIUM for 4 minutes or until thickened. Stir frequently. Add the spinach and its cooking liquid to the soup, and purée in a food processor until smooth. Stir in the cheese, reserving 1 tbsp. Re-heat on MEDIUM for 1 minute. Sprinkle the reserved cheese on top to serve.
To serve 2 people, double the ingredients and cook the soup for 5-6 minutes on MEDIUM.

This page: Consommé with Vegetable Noodles. Facing page: Cheesy Spinach Soup (top) and Tomato and Basil Soup (bottom).

Microwave
COOKING FOR 1 & 2

SNACKS

Italian Ham Sandwiches

PREPARATION TIME: 10 minutes

MICROWAVE COOKING TIME:
4 minutes

SERVES: 2 people

¼ lb Parma, or other Italian ham
2oz sliced mozzarella cheese
4 mild Italian peppers
1 tbsp butter or margarine
Pinch garlic powder
Pinch of oregano
2 French rolls

Mix the butter, garlic and oregano.
Split the rolls and spread the butter
thinly on each of the cut sides. Layer
the ham, peppers and cheese on the
bottom half of the roll. Place the top
on and press down. Place the
sandwiches on a paper towel in the
oven. Cook on MEDIUM for 4-5
minutes or until the cheese melts.
Serve immediately.

Sloppy Joes

PREPARATION TIME: 15 minutes

MICROWAVE COOKING TIME:
14 minutes

SERVES: 2 people

½ lb ground beef or pork
1 small onion, finely chopped
¼ cup chopped green pepper
1 cup tomato sauce
2 tsps Worcestershire sauce

**This page: Italian Ham
Sandwiches (top) and Cheese and
Mushroom Croissants (bottom).
Facing page: Sausage and
Sauerkraut Sandwiches (top) and
Sloppy Joes (bottom).**

½ tsp dry mustard
1½ tsps cider vinegar
1 tsp brown sugar
Salt and pepper
2 Kaiser rolls or hamburger buns

Mix the meat and onion in a casserole and cook, uncovered, for 7 minutes on HIGH. Mash the meat with a fork several times while cooking, to break it up into small pieces. Strain off any fat. Add the remaining ingredients and stir well. Cover and cook for a further 5 minutes on HIGH, stirring occasionally. Wrap the rolls in paper towels and heat for 1-2 minutes on MEDIUM. Split and fill with the Sloppy Joe filling. Mixture freezes well.

Tacos

PREPARATION TIME: 15 minutes
MICROWAVE COOKING TIME: 6 minutes
SERVES: 2 people

4 taco shells
¼ lb ground beef
¼ cup chopped onion
1 tbsp raisins
1 tbsp pine nuts
1 tbsp corn
1 tsp chili powder
¼ cup tomato sauce
Salt and pepper

TOPPINGS
½ cup grated cheese
½ cup sour cream
½ cup chopped tomatoes
1 cup shredded lettuce
1 chopped avocado

Put the beef and onion into a 1 quart casserole. Break the meat up well with a fork. Cover and cook for 2 minutes on HIGH, stirring occasionally to break into small pieces. Drain any fat from the meat and add salt and pepper, chili powder, corn, nuts, raisins and tomato sauce. Cover and cook on MEDIUM for 4 minutes. Spoon into the taco shells and serve with the various toppings.

Sausage and Sauerkraut Sandwiches

PREPARATION TIME: 10 minutes
MICROWAVE COOKING TIME: 1½ minutes
SERVES: 2 people

4 slices rye bread, light or dark
¼ lb smoked sausage (kielbasa or bratwurst), thinly sliced
4 slices Muenster or Tilsit cheese
½ cup drained sauerkraut
2 tbsps butter or margarine

DRESSING
1 tbsp spicy brown mustard
2 tbsps mayonnaise
1½ tsps chopped dill pickle

Melt the butter for 30 seconds on HIGH in a small bowl. Mix dressing and spread on both sides of the bread slices. Layer on the sauerkraut, sausage and cheese. Heat a browning dish for 5 minutes on HIGH. Brush 1 side of the bread with melted butter and place the sandwich in the dish. Cook for 15 seconds, or until golden brown. Turn over and brush the other side with butter and cook that side for 20-30 seconds or until the bread is browned and the cheese melted. Serve hot.

Cheese and Mushroom Croissants

PREPARATION TIME: 15 minutes
MICROWAVE COOKING TIME: 3 minutes
SERVES: 1 person

1 croissant or crescent roll
1 tsp butter
½ tsp flour
2 mushrooms, sliced
¼ cup Gruyère cheese
¼ cup milk
1 tbsp white wine
½ tsp Dijon mustard
Nutmeg
Salt and pepper

Split the top of the croissant, taking care not to cut through to the bottom or the ends. Melt ½ tsp butter in a small bowl for 15 seconds on HIGH. Add the mushrooms and cook for 30 seconds on HIGH and set aside. Melt the remaining butter in a 1 pint measure. Stir in the flour and add the milk and wine gradually. Add a pinch of nutmeg, mustard and salt and pepper. Cook on HIGH for 1 minute or until thick. Stir in the cheese and spoon into the croissant. Top with the mushrooms and heat through for 1 minute on MEDIUM. Serve immediately.

Pizza Muffins

PREPARATION TIME: 10 minutes
MICROWAVE COOKING TIME: 2 minutes
SERVES: 1 person

1 English muffin, split
2 tbsps tomato paste
2 tbsps water
1 green onion, sliced
¼ tsp oregano
Pinch garlic powder
¼ cup pepperoni or Italian salami, chopped, or 4 anchovies
2-3 Italian olives, stoned and halved
1 tsp capers
⅓ cup grated mozzarella cheese
1 tbsp Parmesan cheese
Salt and pepper

Mix the tomato paste with the water, salt and pepper, onion, oregano and garlic powder, and spread on the muffin halves. Arrange the sausage or a cross of anchovies on top. Add the olives and capers and sprinkle on the mozzarella cheese. Sprinkle on the Parmesan cheese last and put the pizzas on a paper towel, then cook for 1½-2 minutes on HIGH. Turn the pizzas once or twice during cooking. For 2 people, double the ingredients and cook for 4-4½ minutes on HIGH.

Facing page: Tacos.

Vegetable Pockets

PREPARATION TIME: 10 minutes

MICROWAVE COOKING TIME:
4-5 minutes

SERVES: 2 people

1 piece whole-wheat pitta bread
1 tbsp olive oil
1 tsp lemon juice
1 tomato, roughly chopped
1 red onion, thinly sliced or 2 green onions,
  sliced
1 green pepper, thinly sliced
1 cup fresh spinach leaves
½ tsp chives
1 tbsp fresh basil leaves, if available
1 small zucchini, thinly sliced
6 black olives, stoned
¼ cup crumbled feta cheese
Salt and pepper

Cut the pitta bread in half and open
out the pockets. Mix the lemon juice
and oil together with the salt and
pepper. Toss the cheese, tomato,
vegetables, herbs and olives together
in the dressing. Fill the pockets with
the vegetables and heat for 4-5
minutes on MEDIUM. Serve
immediately.

Tuna Melt

PREPARATION TIME: 10 minutes

MICROWAVE COOKING TIME:
2 minutes

SERVES: 1 person

1 English muffin, split
1 small can white tuna
2 tbsps cottage cheese
2 tbsps mayonnaise
1 stick celery, chopped
1 tsp chopped parsley
2 tsps chopped chives
½ tsp lemon juice
Alfalfa sprouts
¼ cup grated Colby cheese
Salt and pepper

Mix together the tuna, cottage
cheese, mayonnaise, celery, parsley,
chives, and salt and pepper. Taste and
add lemon juice if desired. Put alfalfa
sprouts on the muffin halves and
spoon on the tuna mixture. Top with

the cheese and heat for 1 minute on
MEDIUM. Increase the heat to
HIGH and heat for 1 minute further,
turning once or twice during cooking.
Serve immediately.

Pocketful of Shrimp

PREPARATION TIME: 10 minutes

MICROWAVE COOKING TIME:
2-4 minutes

SERVES: 2 people

1 piece pitta bread, cut in half
½ cup bean sprouts
½ cup cooked shrimp, peeled and de-
  veined
1 tbsp chili sauce
2 tbsps mayonnaise
½ tsp horseradish

**This page: Pizza Muffins (top) and
Tuna Melt (bottom). Facing page:
Pocketful of Shrimp (top) and
Vegetable Pockets (bottom).**

1 stick celery, chopped
1 ripe avocado, peeled and thickly sliced
1 tbsp lemon juice
Salt and pepper

Cut the pitta bread in half and open
a pocket in each half. Toss the
avocado slices in lemon juice and
place them in the sides of the
pockets. Fill each pocket with bean
sprouts. Mix the shrimp, chili sauce,
mayonnaise, horseradish, salt, pepper
and chopped celery together. Put on
top of the bean sprouts and heat
through for 2-4 minutes on
MEDIUM. Serve immediately.

EGG AND CHEESE

Pipérade

PREPARATION TIME: 10 minutes

MICROWAVE COOKING TIME:
6 minutes, plus 1 minute standing
time

SERVES: 1 person

1 tbsp finely chopped onion
½ tbsp butter
½ cap pimento, finely chopped
1 tomato
Pinch garlic powder
2 eggs
Pinch oregano
Salt and pepper

Put 2 cups water into a bowl and
cover with pierced plastic wrap. Heat
for 3 minutes on HIGH or until
boiling. Put in the tomato and leave
for 30 seconds. Peel and seed the
tomato, and chop roughly. Put the
butter into a medium-sized bowl with
the garlic powder and onion. Cook
on HIGH for 3 minutes. Add the
pimento, tomato and oregano. Cook
on HIGH for 1 minute. Beat the eggs,
salt and pepper together, and add to
the bowl. Cook on HIGH for about
2 minutes, stirring every 30 seconds,
or until the eggs are softly scrambled.
Leave to stand for 1 minute before
serving. Serve on buttered toast or
English muffins, or with French
bread.

Sunrise Scramble

PREPARATION TIME: 15 minutes

MICROWAVE COOKING TIME:
5 minutes, plus 1 minute standing
time

SERVES: 1 person

2 tbsps ham, finely chopped
2 eggs
1 tbsp butter
1 tbsp grated cheese
¼ cup mushrooms, sliced
1 tomato
1 tbsp chopped parsley
Salt and pepper

Put the butter into a small bowl, add
the mushrooms, and cook for 2
minutes on HIGH or until soft.
Drain away any excess liquid. Add
the ham, and cook for 1 minute on
HIGH. Cut the tomato in quarters,
but leave attached at the base. Heat
for 1 minute on HIGH, and keep
warm. Beat the eggs and add the
cheese, parsley, and salt and pepper.
Add the eggs to the bowl with the
ham and mushrooms, and cook for
2 minutes on HIGH, stirring every
30 seconds until softly scrambled.
Leave to stand for 1 minute. Fill the
tomato with the egg mixture and
serve.

Spinach and Cheese Layered Quiche

PREPARATION TIME: 20 minutes

MICROWAVE COOKING TIME:
11-14 minutes, plus 6 minutes
standing time

SERVES: 2 people

PASTRY
⅓ cup all-purpose flour
⅓ cup whole-wheat flour
¼ cup margarine
2 tbsps shortening
¼ cup ice cold water
Pinch of salt

FILLING
½ cup shredded Gruyère or Swiss cheese
3 eggs
¼ cup half and half
¼ cup chopped frozen spinach, well
    drained
Nutmeg
Cayenne pepper or Tabasco
Salt and pepper

Put the flours, salt, margarine and
shortening into the bowl of a food
processor and work until the mixture
resembles fine breadcrumbs. With
the machine running, add the water
gradually until the dough holds
together. It may not be necessary to
add all the water. Roll out the pastry
on a floured board to ⅛″ thick, and
put into a 7″ pie plate. Trim the edge
and flute. Refrigerate for 10 minutes.
Mix the eggs, cheese, half and half
and salt and pepper together well.
Divide the mixture in half: add the
spinach and pinch of nutmeg to one
half, and a pinch of Cayenne pepper
or a dash of Tabasco to the other.
Prick the base of the pastry with a
fork and cook on HIGH for 2-3
minutes or until it starts to crisp.
Pour in the cheese mixture and cook
for 4 minutes on MEDIUM, or until
softly set. Leave to stand for
1 minute. Pour on the spinach
mixture and cook for a further 7-10
minutes or until the center is softly
set. Leave to stand for 6 minutes
before serving.

**Facing page: Sunrise Scramble
(top) and Pipérade (bottom).**

Niçoise Eggs

PREPARATION TIME: 10 minutes

MICROWAVE COOKING TIME:
9 minutes

SERVES: 2 person

2 eggs
4 tomatoes, peeled, seeded and chopped
1 tsp butter
2 mushrooms, chopped
2 tbsps white wine
1 tbsp capers
4 black olives, stoned and sliced
2 anchovies, chopped
1 tbsp tarragon
Pinch of paprika
Salt and pepper
¼ cup Gruyère or Swiss cheese, grated

Put the butter into a small casserole

This page: Italian Fondue (left) and Niçoise Eggs (right). Facing page: Tuna and Tomato Quiche (top) and Spinach and Cheese Layered Quiche (bottom).

and melt for 30 seconds on HIGH. Add the chopped mushrooms, tarragon and half the wine, and cook for 2 minutes on HIGH. Add the remaining ingredients except the cheese, eggs and paprika, and cook for 1-2 minutes on HIGH. Divide the tomato mixture into 2 custard cups and make a well in the center. Put an egg into the center of the mixture in each cup. Pierce the yolk with a sharp knife. Pour over the remaining wine. Cook for 3 minutes on HIGH or until the white is set and yolk is still

soft. Sprinkle on the cheese and paprika and cook for 1 minute on LOW to melt the cheese.

Italian Fondue

PREPARATION TIME: 10 minutes

MICROWAVE COOKING TIME:
5 minutes

SERVES: 1 person

1 cup shredded mozzarella cheese
½ cup shredded mild Cheddar cheese
1 tsp cornstarch
⅓ cup red wine
1 tbsp tomato paste
1 tsp dry vermouth
½ clove garlic, crushed

½ tsp basil
½ tsp oregano
1 French roll, cut into cubes, or broccoli
    flowerets, carrot sticks and celery sticks

Toss the cheese and cornstarch to mix. Put the wine into a deep bowl and cook on MEDIUM for 1-2 minutes, or until it begins to bubble – do not allow it to boil. Add the remaining ingredients except the bread (or vegetables), and stir well to blend completely. Cook for a further 2-3 minutes on MEDIUM, or until the cheese melts. Stir every few seconds. If the mixture begins to boil, reduce the setting to LOW. Serve with the bread cubes or vegetables. Re-heat on LOW if necessary. Serve as an appetizer or as an entrée with a tossed salad.
To serve 2 people, double the ingredients. Cook the wine for 2-3 minutes on MEDIUM, and the cheese and other ingredients for 3-4 minutes on MEDIUM.

Tuna and Tomato Quiche

PREPARATION TIME: 20 minutes

MICROWAVE COOKING TIME: 18 minutes, plus 6 minutes standing time

SERVES: 2 people

PASTRY
⅔ cup all-purpose flour
¼ cup margarine
2 tbsps shortening
1 tbsp paprika
Pinch of salt
¼ cup ice cold water

FILLING
1 can (about 6oz) white tuna, drained
    and flaked
3 eggs
2 tomatoes, peeled
½ cup shredded Cheddar cheese
¼ cup half and half
1 tbsp chopped green onion
Salt and pepper

TOPPING
1 tbsp dry, seasoned breadcrumbs
2 tbsps grated Parmesan cheese

Put the flour, salt, paprika, margarine and shortening into the bowl of a food processor and work until the mixture resembles fine breadcrumbs. With the machine running, add the water gradually until the dough holds together. It may not be necessary to add all the water. Roll out the pastry on a floured board to ⅛″ thick and put into a 7″ pie plate. Trim the edge and flute. Refrigerate for 10 minutes. Beat the eggs with the salt, pepper and half and half. Add the cheese, onion and tuna. Cut the tomatoes into quarters and take out the seeds. Prick the base of the pastry and cook on HIGH for 2-3 minutes, or until starting to crisp. Pour the filling into the pastry shell and decorate the top with the tomatoes. Cook on MEDIUM for 10-15 minutes. Mix the topping ingredients and sprinkle over the top of the quiche 5 minutes before the end of baking. Left-over quiche can be refrigerated for up to 2 days. Eat cold or re-heat on MEDIUM for 2 minutes.

Ham, Broccoli and Pineapple au Gratin

PREPARATION TIME: 15 minutes

MICROWAVE COOKING TIME: 10-12 minutes

SERVES: 2 people

4 slices cooked ham
8 broccoli spears

broccoli for 3 minutes on HIGH. Once assembled, cook for 2-3 minutes on MEDIUM. Left-over cheese sauce can be frozen, or kept in the refrigerator for 2 days. Bring to room temperature, re-heat on MEDIUM for 1-2 minutes to serve the sauce.

Asparagus and Tomato Omelette

| **PREPARATION TIME:** 15 minutes |
| **MICROWAVE COOKING TIME:** 15 minutes |
| **SERVES:** 2 people |

4 eggs, separated
½ cup chopped asparagus, fresh or frozen
2 tbsps water
2 tomatoes, peeled, seeded and chopped
⅓ cup Gruyère cheese, grated
⅓ cup milk
1 tbsp butter or margarine
1 tsp flour
Salt and pepper

Put the asparagus and water into a 1 pint casserole. Cover and cook for 5-6 minutes on HIGH. Beat the egg yolks, milk, flour, and salt and pepper together. Beat the egg whites until stiff but not dry and fold into the yolks. Melt the butter in a 9″ pie plate for 30 seconds on HIGH. Pour the omelette mixture onto the plate and cook on MEDIUM for 7 minutes or until set. Lift the edges of the omelette to allow the uncooked mixture to spread evenly. Sprinkle with the cheese, and spread on the asparagus and chopped tomato. Fold over and cook for 1 minute on LOW to melt the cheese. Serve immediately.

¼ cup sliced mushrooms
1 tbsp butter
4 pineapple rings, drained
2 tbsps water
Pinch of salt
1 tsp dark brown sugar

SAUCE
1 tbsp flour
1 tbsp butter
¼ tsp dry mustard
½ cup milk
2 tbsps shredded Cheddar cheese
Salt and pepper

TOPPING
¼ cup dry seasoned breadcrumbs

Put 1 tbsp butter in a small bowl and cook for 30 seconds on HIGH. Add the mushrooms and cook for 1 minute on HIGH and set aside. Put the broccoli spears into a casserole with the water and a pinch of salt.

Cover and cook for 4 minutes on HIGH. Leave covered while preparing the sauce. In a 2 cup measure, melt 1 tbsp butter for 30 seconds on HIGH. Stir in the flour, mustard, salt and pepper. Add the milk gradually and cook on HIGH for 1-2 minutes, stirring frequently until thick. Stir in the cheese. Put 2 broccoli spears on each ham slice, stalks towards the middle, and top each with the mushrooms. Roll up and put seam-side down in a baking dish. Arrange pineapple rings on each side and sprinkle with the dark brown sugar. Coat the cheese sauce over the broccoli and ham rolls and top with the crumbs. Cook on MEDIUM for 3-4 minutes or until hot. Serve immediately.
To serve 1 person, make full quantity sauce and cut all other ingredients to half quantity. Cook the mushrooms for 30 seconds on HIGH and the

This page: Ham, Broccoli, and Pineapple au Gratin. Facing page: Asparagus and Tomato Omelette.

Egg Foo Yung

PREPARATION TIME: 15 minutes

MICROWAVE COOKING TIME:
10 minutes

SERVES: 2 people

CRAB PATTIES
½ cup frozen crabmeat, defrosted
1 tbsp chopped green pepper
1 tbsp chopped green onion
¼ cup chopped mushrooms
1 small clove garlic, crushed
½ cup bean sprouts
2 eggs, beaten
¼ tsp ground ginger
Salt and pepper

SAUCE
½ cup chicken bouillon
1 tsp sherry
1 tbsp soy sauce
1 tsp oyster sauce (optional)
½ tsp brown sugar
2 tsps cornstarch

Beat the eggs in a medium-sized bowl and stir in the remaining ingredients for the patties. Cook on HIGH for 2 minutes, stirring frequently, until softly set. Heat a browning dish on HIGH for 5 minutes. Pour the mixture into the hot dish in ½ cup amounts, and cook for about 30 seconds per side on HIGH. Cover and keep warm. Combine the sauce ingredients in a 2 cup measure and cook for 1-2 minutes, stirring frequently until clear and thickened. Pour over the patties and serve immediately.

RICE, PASTA AND GRAINS

Bulgur and Spicy Lamb

PREPARATION TIME: 20 minutes
MICROWAVE COOKING TIME: 26 minutes
SERVES: 2 people

1 cup bulgur wheat
1 cup water
1 small onion, finely chopped
¼ lb ground lamb
¼ tsp oil
1 cup canned plum tomatoes
1 tsp cumin
¼ tsp cinnamon
1 tsp chopped mint
2 tbsps raisins
2 tbsps almonds, chopped
¼ cup yogurt
1 egg
Salt and pepper
1 bay leaf

Put the bulgur and water into a 2 quart casserole with a pinch of salt. Cover and cook on HIGH for 5 minutes, and leave covered while preparing the rest of the ingredients. Heat a browning dish for 5 minutes on HIGH. Put in the oil, add the onion and lamb, breaking the latter up into small pieces with a fork. Add the cumin, cinnamon, and salt and pepper. Return the dish to the oven and cook for 5 minutes on HIGH, stirring frequently. Add the tomatoes, mint, bay leaf, and salt and pepper. Cover and cook for 5 minutes on HIGH. Add the raisins and almonds, and leave to stand. Drain the bulgur wheat well, pressing to remove excess moisture. Mix with the egg and yogurt. Add salt and pepper and put half the bulgur in the bottom of a baking dish. Spread with the lamb filling and cover with another layer of bulgur. Cook uncovered for 5-6 minutes on MEDIUM. Leave to stand, to firm up, for 5 minutes before serving. Serve with a cucumber and yogurt salad.

Facing page: Egg Foo Yung. This page: Polenta with Pepper and Leek Salad (top) and Bulgur and Spicy Lamb (bottom).

To serve 1 person, prepare the full quantity casserole and divide into two. One of the casseroles may be frozen.

Sausage Risotto

PREPARATION TIME: 15 minutes

MICROWAVE COOKING TIME: 29 minutes

SERVES: 2 people

½ cup Italian rice, uncooked
¼ cup broken, uncooked spaghetti
1 Italian sausage, mild or hot
1 tbsp oil
1 small onion, finely sliced
½ clove garlic, crushed
½ cup quartered mushrooms
2 tomatoes, peeled and seeded
1½ tsps chopped parsley
½ tsp basil
1 cup beef bouillon
¼ cup Parmesan cheese
Salt and pepper

Remove sausage meat from casing. Heat a browning dish for 5 minutes on HIGH. Add the oil and sausage. Cook for 4 minutes on HIGH, breaking up the sausage meat with the fork. Add the onion, garlic and mushrooms, and cook for 2 minutes more on HIGH, stirring frequently. Put the contents of the browning dish into a 1 quart casserole and add the rice, spaghetti, basil, salt and pepper, and beef bouillon. Cover and cook for 15 minutes on HIGH. Stir in the parsley and chopped tomatoes, and leave to stand 3 minutes before serving. Sprinkle with Parmesan cheese.

Tri-colored Tagliatelle and Vegetables

PREPARATION TIME: 10 minutes

MICROWAVE COOKING TIME: 12 minutes, plus 2 minutes standing time

SERVES: 1 person

2oz tagliatelle or fettucini (mixture of red, green and plain)
½ a small sweet red pepper, cut into ¼" strips
½ a small onion, thinly sliced
½ cup broccoli flowerets
2 tbsps butter
1 small clove garlic, crushed
1½ tsps dried rosemary (or 1 sprig fresh)
Grated Parmesan cheese
Salt and pepper

Put the pasta into a large bowl and cover with water. Cook for 6 minutes on HIGH. Leave to stand for 2 minutes. Rinse in hot water and leave to drain. If using fresh pasta, cut the cooking time in half. Put 1 tbsp butter into a medium-sized bowl and add the broccoli, onion and

This page: Sausage Risotto. Facing page: Tri-colored Tagliatelle and Vegetables.

red pepper strips. Cover with pierced plastic wrap and cook for 1-2 minutes on HIGH. Toss with the pasta and keep warm. Melt the remaining butter with the crushed garlic and rosemary for 30 seconds on HIGH in a small bowl or custard cup. Strain the butter onto the pasta and vegetables and discard the rosemary and garlic. Season with salt and pepper. Heat the pasta through on MEDIUM for 2 minutes. Toss with Parmesan cheese and serve.

For 2 people, double all the ingredients. Cook the pasta for 10 minutes on HIGH if using dried, and 5 minutes on HIGH if using fresh. Cook the broccoli, onion and red pepper for 2-3 minutes on HIGH.

Polenta with Pepper and Leek Salad

PREPARATION TIME: 15 minutes

MICROWAVE COOKING TIME: 12 minutes, plus 5 minutes standing time

SERVES: 2 people

½ cup yellow cornmeal
1½ cups water
1 tbsp finely chopped onion
¼ cup shredded mozzarella cheese
¼ cup Parmesan cheese
Salt and pepper

SALAD
1 red pepper
1 large or 2 small leeks

DRESSING
1 tbsp vinegar
2 tbsps oil
½ tsp dry mustard
¼ tsp sugar
¼ tsp fennel seeds, crushed
¼ tsp marjoram

Mix the cornmeal, salt and pepper, onion and water in a large bowl. Cook for 6 minutes on HIGH. Add the mozzarella, cover and leave to stand for 5 minutes. Spread into a square pan and sprinkle the top with the Parmesan cheese. Refrigerate, and when ready to use, cut into squares and heat for 1 minute on HIGH before serving. Slice the pepper into ¼" strips. Trim off the dark green tops of the leeks and slice the white part into quarters. Mix the dressing ingredients together and put the vegetables into a 1 pint casserole. Pour over the dressing and mix together well. Cover and cook for 5 minutes on MEDIUM. Serve warm with the polenta.

Barley Ring with Turkey Filling

PREPARATION TIME: 20 minutes

MICROWAVE COOKING TIME: 31 minutes, plus 5 minutes standing time

SERVES: 2 people

1 cup pearl barley
3 cups water
1 egg, beaten
½ cup whole cranberries
½ tsp sugar
Grated rind and juice of half an orange
½ cup chopped walnuts
2 tbsps butter or margarine
1 shallot
¾ cup mushrooms, sliced
½ lb uncooked boned turkey, cut into 1" pieces
1 tbsp flour
½ cup chicken bouillon
2 tbsps parsley
½ cup cream
Salt and pepper

Put the barley into a large bowl with the water and a pinch of salt. Cover with pierced plastic wrap and cook for 20 minutes on HIGH, stirring once. Leave to stand, covered, for at least 5 minutes. Combine the cranberries, sugar and orange juice in a small bowl. Cook uncovered for 1-2 minutes on HIGH. Drain the barley well, and fold in the parsley, cranberries, walnuts, orange rind and beaten egg. Press into a 2 cup microwave ring-mold. Put the butter into a 2 cup casserole and cook for 30 seconds on HIGH to melt. Add the turkey, shallot and mushrooms. Cover and cook for 2 minutes on HIGH, stirring every 30 seconds. Sprinkle on the flour and stir in well. Add the stock and cream and blend well. Season, cover and cook for an additional 3 minutes on HIGH, stirring every 30 seconds until thickened. Keep warm. Re-heat the barley ring covered with pierced plastic wrap for 3 minutes on HIGH. Turn it out and fill the center with the turkey.
To serve one person, cut all the ingredients to half quantity, and omit the egg. Serve the barley as a pilaff topped with the turkey filling.

Indian Pilaff

PREPARATION TIME: 15 minutes

MICROWAVE COOKING TIME: 30 minutes

SERVES: 2 people

½ cup long-grain rice (basmati, if available)
¼ cup almonds, toasted
1 small onion, sliced
1 tbsp oil
2 tbsps peas
2 okra, sliced
2 tbsps coconut
2 tbsps golden raisins
1 cup chicken bouillon
1 tbsp lemon juice
1 tbsp curry powder
1 tbsp chopped parsley
½ tsp dried red pepper flakes
Salt and pepper

Heat a browning dish for 5 minutes on HIGH. Sprinkle on the almonds and return the dish to the oven. Cook on HIGH for 3 minutes, stirring the almonds every 30 seconds until golden brown. Remove the almonds from the dish and allow to cool. Add the oil to the browning dish and stir in the sliced onion. Return to the oven and cook for 2 minutes on HIGH or until golden brown. Add the curry powder and cook for 1 minute on HIGH. Put the onion into a casserole and add the rice, pepper flakes, coconut, chicken bouillon and lemon juice. Cover and cook on HIGH for 3 minutes until boiling. Reduce the setting to MEDIUM, add the raisins and cook for 12 minutes. Add the peas, okra and parsley 2 minutes before the end of the cooking time. Sprinkle with toasted almonds before serving. (One serving may be kept in the refrigerator for 2 days. Re-heat for 2-3 minutes on MEDIUM.)

Facing page: Barley Ring with Turkey Filling.

Fried Rice

PREPARATION TIME: 15 minutes

MICROWAVE COOKING TIME:
12 minutes

SERVES: 2 people

½ cup quick-cooking rice
¾ cup water
3 dried Chinese mushrooms
2 green onions, sliced
¼ cup shrimp, peeled and de-veined
Small piece ginger root
Small can sliced bamboo shoots or lotus
    root
1 egg
1½ tsps soy sauce
½ tsp sesame oil
1 tbsp vegetable oil
Salt and pepper

Put the mushrooms into a bowl with enough water to cover. Cover with pierced plastic wrap and cook for 3 minutes on HIGH. Leave to stand until softened. Put the rice, water and a pinch of salt in a 1 quart casserole. Cover and cook on HIGH for 2½ minutes. Leave to stand while preparing the other ingredients. Drain and slice the mushrooms. Slice the ginger into thin slivers. Beat the egg with the soy sauce. Heat a browning dish for 5 minutes on HIGH, pour in the vegetable oil and quickly add the mushrooms, bamboo shoots, ginger, and half the onion. Stir and return to the oven, and cook for 1 minute on HIGH. Mix the rice with the egg, soy sauce and sesame oil, and stir into the mixture in the browning dish. Cook, uncovered, for 3 minutes on HIGH, stirring every 30 seconds until the egg sets. Add the shrimp after 2 minutes. Serve garnished with the remaining green onion.

Clam Shells in Saffron Sauce

PREPARATION TIME: 15 minutes

MICROWAVE COOKING TIME:
16 minutes, plus 5 minutes
standing time

SERVES: 2 people

1½ cups whole-wheat
1 cup canned whole clams, liquid
    reserved
2 tbsps chopped parsley
1-2 tomatoes, peeled, seeded and cut into
    ¼" strips
1 shallot, finely chopped
1 tbsp saffron
1 tbsp butter
½ tbsp flour
½ cup heavy cream
Reserved clam juice, made up to ½ cup
    with water if necessary

2 tbsps white wine
Salt and pepper

Put the pasta shells into a large bowl with enough hot water to cover. Cook for 8 minutes on HIGH and leave to stand for 5 minutes. Rinse under hot water and leave in cold water. Melt the butter in a small bowl on HIGH for 30 seconds. Stir in the flour and add the clam juice gradually. Add the wine, shallot and saffron and cook, covered with

SAUCE

1½ cups canned plum tomatoes
1 tbsp oil
½ cup sliced mushrooms
½ clove garlic, crushed
¼ tsp basil
Pinch ground allspice
1 tsp tomato paste
1 bay leaf
Salt and pepper

FILLING

½ cup frozen chopped spinach, defrosted
¼ cup pepperoni sausage, skinned and
    chopped
1 cup ricotta cheese
¼ cup grated Parmesan cheese (plus extra
    for serving if desired)
Nutmeg
Salt and pepper

Put the cannelloni or large shell pasta into a large, shallow casserole, and pour over enough hot water to cover. Cook for 8 minutes on HIGH. Leave to stand for 5 minutes. Rinse in hot water and leave standing in cold water. Put the oil into a 1 quart casserole and heat for 30 seconds on HIGH. Add the mushrooms and garlic and cook for 1 minute on HIGH. Add the remaining sauce ingredients, cover, and cook for 5 minutes on HIGH. Stir well and mash the tomatoes to break them up. Meanwhile drain the pasta well. Mix the filling ingredients together and fill the pasta. Put the pasta into a small casserole dish and pour over the tomato sauce. Cook on HIGH for 5 minutes to heat through. Serve with additional Parmesan cheese. To serve one person, halve the quantity of each ingredient. Cook the sauce for 3 minutes total in a smaller casserole or bowl. Alternatively, prepare this recipe in full and freeze one half for later use.

pierced plastic wrap, for 3 minutes on HIGH until thickenend. Stir every 30 seconds. Stir in the cream and cook for 1 minute on HIGH. Mix in the clams, parsley, and salt and pepper. Cover and cook for 2 minutes on HIGH to heat through. Add the tomato strips and cook for 1 minute on MEDIUM. Pour over the pasta and serve immediately. To serve 1 person, cut the quantity of all the ingredients by half. Cook the sauce for half of the recommended time.

Cannelloni Stuffed with Spinach, Cheese and Pepperoni

PREPARATION TIME: 15 minutes

MICROWAVE COOKING TIME:
19 minutes, plus 5 minutes standing time

SERVES: 2 people

6-8 (depending on size) cannelloni or large shell pasta

Facing page: Indian Pilaff (top) and Fried Rice (bottom). This page: Clam Shells in Saffron Sauce (top) and Cannelloni Stuffed with Spinach, Cheese and Pepperoni (bottom).

FISH AND SEAFOOD

Stuffed Trout

PREPARATION TIME: 15 minutes

MICROWAVE COOKING TIME:
5 minutes

SERVES: 1 person

1 whole rainbow trout, cleaned
1 shallot, finely chopped
½ cup frozen chopped spinach, thawed
Pinch of nutmeg
¼ cup flaked crabmeat
1 tbsp chopped hazelnuts
1 cap pimento, chopped
2 tbsps heavy cream
1 tbsp lemon juice
Paprika
Salt and pepper

Put the spinach, nutmeg and shallot into a small bowl. Cover with pierced plastic wrap and cook for 1 minute on HIGH to soften the shallot. Stir in the crab, nuts, paprika, salt, pepper, pimento and cream. Trim the tail and fins of the trout, and spoon the stuffing into the cavity. Sprinkle with lemon juice and cook in a shallow baking dish covered with pierced plastic wrap for 4 minutes on HIGH. Peel the skin off the body of the trout, but leave on the head and tail. Garnish with lemon if desired.

Salmon Steaks Bernaise

PREPARATION TIME: 10 minutes

MICROWAVE COOKING TIME:
4-5 minutes

SERVES: 1 person

1 salmon steak

1 tbsp lemon juice
Salt and pepper

SAUCE
2 egg yolks
1 tsp tarragon or white wine vinegar
1 tsp lemon juice
1 tsp chopped tarragon
1 tsp chopped parsley
Cayenne pepper
¼ cup butter, melted

This page: Portuguese Seafood Stew. Facing page: Salmon Steaks Bernaise (top) and Stuffed Trout (bottom).

Have a bowl of ice water ready. Combine the egg yolks, vinegar, lemon juice and herbs in a 1 pint glass measure. In a small bowl, melt the butter for 1 minute on HIGH until very hot. Whisk it into the egg yolks. Cook on HIGH for 15 seconds and

whisk again. Repeat the process until the sauce is thick: this usually takes about 2 minutes. Put immediately into the bowl of ice water to stop the cooking. Add the Cayenne pepper, and salt if necessary. If the sauce begins to curdle, put the measure immediately into ice water and beat vigorously. Put the fish into a small baking dish with salt and pepper and lemon juice. Cover with pierced plastic wrap and cook on MEDIUM for 2-3 minutes. Leave to stand, covered, while making the sauce.

Flounder with Avocado

PREPARATION TIME: 15 minutes	
MICROWAVE COOKING TIME: 8 minutes	
SERVES: 2 people	

½ lb flounder fillets, skinned
1 small ripe avocado
2 tbsps cream cheese
1 tsp chives
Juice of 1 lime (or of half a lemon)
1 tbsp white wine
1 tsp butter
½ tsp flour
½ cup heavy cream
Salt and pepper

GARNISH
Reserved chives
Reserved avocado slices

Reserve 2-4 thin slices of avocado and brush with the lemon or lime juice. Mash the rest of the avocado with the cream cheese, chives, salt and pepper, and 1 tsp lime or lemon juice. Spread the filling over the fish and fold each fillet in half. Put the fillets in a shallow casserole and pour over the wine and remaining juice. Cover with pierced plastic wrap and cook for 6 minutes on MEDIUM. Keep warm. In a small bowl, melt the butter for 30 seconds on HIGH and stir in the flour. Strain on the cooking liquid from the fish and add the cream. Cook, uncovered, for 2 minutes on HIGH until thickened. Remove the fish to serve on plates and pour some of the sauce over

each fillet. Garnish with the reserved avocado slices and chives.

Lemon and Almond Sole

PREPARATION TIME: 10 minutes	
MICROWAVE COOKING TIME: 11 minutes	
SERVES: 2 people	

2 whole sole fillets
1 lemon
2 tbsps butter
½ cup almonds
¼ cup cornflake crumbs
2-4 parsley sprigs
Salt and pepper

Cut 4 thin slices from the lemon and squeeze the rest for juice. Cut 2 circles of unwaxed paper and grease with 1 tbsp butter. Lay on the fillets of fish and sprinkle over the lemon juice, salt and pepper. Seal up the parcels by twisting the open edges of the paper together. Cook for 5 minutes on MEDIUM. Heat a browning dish on HIGH for 4 minutes and add the remaining butter. Stir in the almonds and cook for 2 minutes, stirring frequently until brown. Stir in the cornflake crumbs. Open the parcels to serve and spoon on the almond topping. Garnish with reserved lemon slices and parsley.

Portuguese Seafood Stew

PREPARATION TIME: 15 minutes	
MICROWAVE COOKING TIME: 11 minutes	
SERVES: 2 people	

3 tomatoes, chopped
½ a green pepper, chopped
½ cup canned clams, in shells if possible, and liquid
1 cod fillet (about ¼ lb), cut into 2" pieces
1 red snapper fillet (about ¼ lb), cut into 2" pieces
4 large raw shrimp, peeled and de-veined, or ½ cup small shrimp

½ a clove garlic, chopped
¼ cup chopped onion
2 tbsps olive oil
1 tsp tomato paste
1 tbsp chopped parsley
6 chopped black olives
½ cup white wine
1 potato, cut into 1" pieces
Salt and pepper

Put the cod and snapper into a casserole. Put the olive oil into another casserole with the onion and garlic and heat for 1 minute on HIGH. Add the potatoes, liquid from the clams, and the wine. Cover and cook for 6 minutes on HIGH. Stir in the tomato paste, add the fish and peppers, and cook for 2 minutes on HIGH. Add the shrimp and cook a further minute on HIGH. Add the tomatoes, clams and olives and cook for another minute on HIGH. Season, and garnish with chopped parsley.

Macadamia Fillets

PREPARATION TIME: 10 minutes	
MICROWAVE COOKING TIME: 5 minutes	
SERVES: 2 people	

2 sole or flounder fillets
1 small can pineapple chunks
¼ of a green pepper, cut into ¼" strips
1 green onion, shredded
⅓ cup Macadamia nuts, roughly chopped

SAUCE
Reserved pineapple juice
1 tbsp honey
2 tsps soy sauce
1 tbsp vinegar
¼ tsp dry mustard
1 tsp cornstarch

Facing page: Flounder with Avocado (top) and Lemon and Almond Sole (bottom).

Drain the pineapple and set aside the chunks. Mix the juice and the other sauce ingredients together in a bowl. Add the green pepper and cook uncovered for 1-2 minutes on HIGH or until thickened, stirring every 30 seconds. Add the pineapple chunks, nuts and onions, and set aside. Put the fish into a shallow casserole, thinner portion towards the center of the dish. Cover with pierced plastic wrap, and cook for 2 minutes on HIGH. Allow to stand for 30 seconds. Remove carefully to serving dishes. Coat with the Macadamia sauce. Serve with fried rice or stir-fried vegetables.

This page: Shrimp and Broccoli au Gratin. Facing page: Macadamia Fillets.

Shrimp and Broccoli au Gratin

PREPARATION TIME:	10 minutes
MICROWAVE COOKING TIME:	6 minutes
SERVES:	2 people

1 cup broccoli flowerets
½ lb large cooked shrimp, peeled and de-veined
2 tbsps Parmesan cheese
1 tbsp dry breadcrumbs
1 tsp paprika

SAUCE
2 tbsps Cheddar cheese
1 tbsp butter
1 tbsp flour
½ cup milk
Pinch of dry mustard
Pinch of Cayenne pepper
Salt and pepper

Melt 1 tbsp butter in a small bowl for

Melt the butter in a 1 pint casserole for 30 seconds on HIGH and add the shallot. Cook for 1 minute on HIGH, add the flour, white wine and saffron, and stir well to mix. Add the scallops (cut in half if large) and cook for 1-2 minutes on HIGH. Stir in the cream, parsley and pepper, and cook for a further 2 minutes on HIGH. Serve on parsley rice.

Lobster in Sherry Cream

PREPARATION TIME: 20 minutes

MICROWAVE COOKING TIME:
4 minutes

SERVES: 2 people

1 whole large lobster, boiled; or 1 large
  lobster tail
½ cup sliced mushrooms
½ tsp celery salt
½ cup heavy cream
2 tbsps sherry
½ tsp butter
½ tsp flour
½ cup Gruyère cheese
Paprika
Pepper

Crack the lobster claws and remove the meat. Remove the meat from the tail, and combine. Reserve the empty tail shell to cook in if desired. Melt the butter for 15 seconds on HIGH, and add the mushrooms. Cook for 1 minute on HIGH and add the flour, sherry, cream, celery salt, and pepper. Cook for 2 more minutes on HIGH until thick, stirring frequently. Add the lobster and spoon into the shell, or a baking dish. Sprinkle on the cheese and plenty of paprika. Cook for 2 minutes on HIGH. Serve immediately.

This page: Scallops in Saffron Cream (top) and Lobster in Sherry Cream (bottom). Facing page: Orange Glazed Lamb Chops with Glazed Vegetables.

30 seconds on HIGH. Stir in the flour, mustard and Cayenne pepper. Add the milk gradually until smooth. Cook for 1-2 minutes on HIGH, stirring every 30 seconds. Add salt and pepper and stir in the Cheddar cheese. Cover and set aside. Put the broccoli in a small bowl with 2 tbsps water. Cover with pierced plastic wrap and cook for 3 minutes on HIGH until almost tender. In individual dishes or 1 large baking dish, scatter over the broccoli and shrimp. Coat over the sauce, and sprinkle on the Parmesan cheese, crumbs and paprika. Heat through for 1-2 minutes on HIGH before serving.

Scallops in Saffron Cream

PREPARATION TIME: 10 minutes

MICROWAVE COOKING TIME:
8 minutes

SERVES: 2 people

2 cups uncooked scallops (or 1 cup, if very
  large)
1 shallot, finely chopped
1 small red pepper cut into ¼″ strips
1 tsp parsley
1 tsp saffron
½ cup white wine
1½ tbsps butter
1½ tbsps flour
½ cup heavy cream

MEAT, POULTRY AND GAME

Orange Glazed Lamb Chops with Glazed Vegetables

PREPARATION TIME: 20 minutes

MICROWAVE COOKING TIME: 14 minutes

SERVES: 2 people

2 lamb shoulder chops
½ cup orange juice
2 tsps dark corn syrup
½ tsp red wine vinegar or cider vinegar
½ tsp cornstarch
1 tbsp water
1 tbsp oil
1 carrot, cut into thick barrel shapes
1 turnip, quartered
½ cup small onions
1 small potato, quartered
1 tbsp butter
Salt and pepper

GARNISH
Orange slices

Heat a browning dish for 5 minutes on HIGH. Put in the oil and chops and cook for 2 minutes on HIGH, turning once, until lightly browned on both sides. Transfer the chops to a casserole dish. Melt the butter and add the vegetables. Cook for 5 minutes on HIGH, stirring frequently to brown evenly. Add to the casserole dish with the chops. De-glaze the browning dish with the orange juice and vinegar, scraping any sediment off the base of the dish. Stir in the corn syrup, salt and pepper, and pour over the chops and vegetables. Cover with pierced plastic wrap and cook on MEDIUM for 6 minutes, or until chops are cooked as much as desired. The chops may be served slightly pink. Remove the chops and vegetables from the casserole and dissolve the cornstarch in the water. Stir into the liquid in the casserole and cook, uncovered, for 1 minute on HIGH or until boiling and clear. Pour over the chops and vegetables and garnish with orange slices.

To serve 1 person, reduce the quantity of each ingredient by half, but cook for the same length of time.

Pheasant in Gin

PREPARATION TIME: 15 minutes

MICROWAVE COOKING TIME:
22 minutes

SERVES: 2 people

1 small pheasant, dressed (about 1½-
    1¾ lbs)
1 apple, peeled and chopped
¼ cup gin
1 tsp juniper berries
½ tsp rosemary
2 tbsps chicken bouillon
1 tbsp butter
1½ tsps flour
1½ cups shredded red cabbage

Heat a browning dish for 5 minutes
on HIGH. Put in the butter and,
when foaming, add the pheasant.
Cook for 3 minutes to lightly brown
all sides of the pheasant, turning four
times while cooking. Transfer to a
medium-sized deep casserole and set
aside. Add flour to the dish and
scrape up any sediment. Cook for
1 minute to lightly brown the flour.
De-glaze the pan with chicken
bouillon and add the casserole with
the remaining ingredients except the
cabbage. Cover and cook for 10
minutes or until the pheasant is
tender. It may be served slightly pink.
During the last 3 minutes, add the
red cabbage. Can be served with the
warm vegetable salad instead of the
red cabbage garnish.
To serve 1 person, prepare the
complete recipe and use half. The
other half will freeze well.

Spicy Steak Kebabs

PREPARATION TIME: 10 minutes,
plus 1 hour to marinate meat

MICROWAVE COOKING TIME:
6 minutes

SERVES: 2 people

½ lb sirloin steak, cut into 1½" cubes
1 leek, white part only
4 large mushrooms
4 cherry tomatoes
½ green pepper, sliced into 1" squares

MARINADE
2 tbsps oil
1 tbsp lemon juice
½ clove garlic, crushed
¼ tsp ground cumin
¼ tsp ground coriander
¼ tsp gravy browning
Pinch Cayenne pepper
Salt and pepper

Mix the marinade ingredients
together and put in the steak cubes,
turning to coat evenly. Leave for 1
hour. Thread the meat and vegetables
onto wooden skewers. Do not pack
the ingredients too tightly together.
Put on a roasting rack and cook on
MEDIUM for about 6 minutes,
turning and basting frequently until
cooked as much as desired. Put
remaining marinade into a smaller
dish and cook for 2-3 minutes on
HIGH until syrupy. Serve on a bed of
rice. Pour the sauce over the cooked
kebabs.
To serve one person, prepare only
half of each ingredient, but cook for
the same length of time.

**This page: Spicy Steak Kebabs.
Facing page: Pheasant in Gin.**

Stuffed Chicken Breasts in Lemon Tarragon Cream

PREPARATION TIME: 15 minutes	
MICROWAVE COOKING TIME: 18 minutes	
SERVES: 2 people	

2 boned chicken breast halves, skinned
1 tsp butter
½ cup finely chopped mushrooms
3oz package cream cheese
2 tbsps white wine
1 tbsp lemon juice
Salt and pepper

SAUCE
1 tbsp butter
½ tbsp flour
Juice of ½ lemon
½ cup chicken stock
¼ cup heavy cream
½ tsp chopped tarragon, fresh or dried
Salt and pepper

GARNISH
Lemon slices

Cut a pocket along the thicker side of each chicken breast half. Melt 1 tbsp butter for 30 seconds on HIGH in a small bowl. Add the white wine, salt and pepper, and mushrooms. Cook, uncovered, for 2 minutes on HIGH to soften the mushrooms. Cook for an additional 1 minute to evaporate liquid if excessive. Mix with the cream cheese and fill the pockets of the chicken. Put the breasts into a small casserole and sprinkle over the lemon juice and about 1 tbsp water. Cover and cook for about 12 minutes on MEDIUM or until white and firm. Keep warm. In a small bowl melt 1 tbsp butter for 30 seconds on HIGH. Stir in the flour and add the stock and lemon juice gradually. Pour in any cooking liquid from the chicken and add the cream and tarragon. Cook for 1-2 minutes on HIGH, stirring every 30 seconds until thickened. Add salt and pepper. Spoon over the chicken breasts to serve and garnish with lemon slices. Serve with French peas or zucchini rolls.
To serve one person, reduce the quantity of each ingredient by half.

Cook the mushroom filling for the same length of time, and the filled chicken breasts for 10 minutes on MEDIUM. Cook the sauce for about 1 minute on HIGH.

Chicken, Ham and Cheese Rolls with Mustard Sauce

PREPARATION TIME: 15 minutes	
MICROWAVE COOKING TIME: 9 minutes	
SERVES: 1 person	

1 chicken breast half, skinned and boned
1 thin slice cooked ham
1 thin slice Swiss cheese
1 tsp chopped capers
1 tsp butter
2½ tbsps cornflake crumbs
¼ tsp paprika
Salt and pepper

SAUCE
1 tbsp butter or margarine
1 tbsp flour
½ cup milk
3 tbsps dry white wine
1 tsp Dijon mustard
1 tsp salad mustard
Salt and pepper

Place the chicken breast between 2 pieces of waxed paper and flatten with a meat mallet to about ⅛″. Lay the cheese on top of the slice of ham. Sprinkle on the capers, and roll up, folding in the sides, and fasten with wooden picks. Melt 1 tsp butter for 30 seconds on HIGH. Combine the cornflake crumbs with the paprika and salt and pepper on a sheet of waxed paper. Brush the chicken with the melted butter and then roll in the crumbs to coat. Push the crumb coating into the surface of the chicken. Put the chicken seam side down into a small casserole dish and cook, uncovered, on MEDIUM for 2 minutes. Turn over, cook for a further 1 minute on MEDIUM, and keep warm while preparing the sauce. Melt ½ tbsp butter for 30 seconds on

HIGH in a small bowl. Stir in the flour and add the milk and wine gradually. Stir in the mustards and salt and pepper. Cook, uncovered, for 1-2 minutes on HIGH, stirring every 30 seconds until thickened. Keep warm. Re-heat the chicken on HIGH for 2 minutes and serve with the sauce.
To serve 2 people, double all the ingredients. Cook the chicken for 4 minutes on MEDIUM and the sauce for 2-3 minutes on HIGH. Re-heat the chicken on HIGH for 2 minutes.

Rabbit with Olives

PREPARATION TIME: 15 minutes	
MICROWAVE COOKING TIME: 23-28 minutes	
SERVES: 2 people	

2 rabbit pieces (hind- or fore-quarters)
2 tbsps butter
2 tsps flour
1 shallot, chopped
¼ cup dry vermouth
¼ cup beef bouillon
½ cup whole mushrooms
¼ tsp oregano
¼ tsp thyme
1 tbsp wholegrain mustard
12 stoned green olives, left whole
¼ cup heavy cream
Salt and pepper

Soak the rabbit overnight to whiten the meat, in enough water to cover, with a squeeze of lemon juice and a pinch of salt. Heat a browning dish for 5 minutes on HIGH. Melt the butter and cook the rabbit pieces for 2 minutes on HIGH, turning over after 1 minute to brown both sides. Remove from the dish to a 1 pint casserole. Add the mushrooms and shallot to the browning dish with the flour. Cook for 1 minute on HIGH to brown lightly. De-glaze the pan with the bouillon and pour the contents over the rabbit. Add the vermouth,

Facing page: Chicken, Ham and Cheese Rolls with Mustard Sauce (top) and Stuffed Chicken Breasts in Lemon Tarragon Cream (bottom).

herbs, mustard, and salt and pepper. Cover and cook on MEDIUM for 15-20 minutes, or until the rabbit is tender. After 10 minutes, add the olives and cream. Serve with rice or noodles.

To serve one person, half the complete recipe will freeze well.

Devilled Cornish Hen with Golden Rice Stuffing

PREPARATION TIME: 20 minutes

MICROWAVE COOKING TIME: 16 minutes

SERVES: 1 person

1 Cornish game hen about 1½ lbs
¼ cup quick-cooking rice
⅓ cup hot water
1 shallot, finely chopped
½ cap pimento, diced
1 tbsp chopped pecans
Pinch saffron
2 tbsps bottled steak sauce
1 tbsp butter
½ tsp paprika
½ tsp dry mustard
½ tsp chili powder
1 tsp sugar
Pinch Cayenne pepper
¼ cup chicken bouillon
Salt and pepper

GARNISH
Small bunch watercress or parsley

Put the rice, saffron, shallot and hot water into a 1 pint casserole, cover, and cook on HIGH for 2 minutes or until the rice is tender and has absorbed all the color from the saffron. Add the pimento and pecans, and allow to cool slightly. Stuff the hen with rice. Mix together the spices, salt and pepper, and sugar. Melt 1 tbsp butter for 30 seconds on HIGH and brush it over the hen. Rub the spices over all surfaces of the hen. Close the cavity with wooden picks and place the hen, breast-side down, on a roasting rack. Combine remaining melted butter with the steak sauce and any remaining spices. Cook the hen for 5 minutes on HIGH and baste with the steak sauce mixture. Turn breast-side up, cook for 5 minutes on HIGH, and baste. Cook for 2 minutes more, or until the juices run clear. Leave to stand for 5 minutes before serving. Add the chicken bouillon to the remaining sauce mixture, re-heat for 1-2 minutes on HIGH and pour over the hen to serve. Garnish with watercress or parsley.

To serve 2 people, double all quantities. Add 5 minutes to the cooking time for the hens.

This page: **Rabbit with Olives (top)** and **Venison Bourguignonne (bottom).** Facing page: **Devilled Cornish Hen with Golden Rice Stuffing.**

Venison Bourguignonne

PREPARATION TIME: 15 minutes

MICROWAVE COOKING TIME: 36 minutes, plus 15 minutes standing time

SERVES: 2 people

½ lb venison from the leg
1 thick-cut slice bacon, cut into ¼" pieces
½ cup small onions
¼ cup mushrooms, quartered
½ clove garlic, crushed
1 tbsp butter
1 tbsp flour
⅓ cup red wine
¾ cup beef bouillon
1 tsp tomato paste
1 bay leaf
¼ tsp thyme
Salt and pepper

Melt the butter for 30 seconds on HIGH in a large casserole. Add the onion, bacon, mushrooms and garlic, and cook for 1 minute on HIGH until slightly brown. Remove from the casserole and set aside. Add the venison and cook for 2-3 minutes on HIGH, stirring occasionally to brown slightly. Sprinkle on the flour, and cook for a further minute on HIGH. Stir in the wine, bouillon and tomato paste. Add the thyme and bay leaf and cover the casserole. Cook, stirring occasionally, for 15 minutes on MEDIUM. Add the remaining ingredients, re-cover the casserole, and cook for another 15 minutes on MEDIUM. Leave to stand for 15 minutes before serving. Serve with boiled potatoes or noodles. To serve one person, cook the full recipe, use half and the other half will freeze well.

Fiery Duck

PREPARATION TIME: 15-20 minutes, plus 30-60 minutes to marinate duck

MICROWAVE COOKING TIME:
8 minutes, plus 1 minute standing time

SERVES: 2 people

½ a duck breast, boned and skinned – about ½ lb. If duck parts are unavailable, cut a whole duck into quarters and freeze the leg portions.
½ a small red pepper, sliced into ¼" strips
2 sticks celery, thinly sliced
1 cup bean sprouts
2 green onions, sliced
½ cup roasted cashew nuts
½-1 tsp Szechuan pepper, or crushed dried chili peppers

½ tsp cornstarch
¼ cup chicken bouillon

MARINADE
2 tsps rice or cider vinegar
2 tsps soy sauce
2 tsps sherry
2 tsps sesame seed oil
Pinch ground ginger
½ clove crushed garlic
Salt and pepper

Remove the skin and bone from the breast portions and cut the duck into thin strips. Combine the marinade ingredients in a medium-sized bowl and stir in the duck pieces. Cover the bowl and chill for 30-60 minutes. Drain the duck, reserving the marinade, and mix the cornstarch, bouillon and Szechuan or chili pepper with the marinade. Put the duck into a large casserole and pour over sauce. Stir to mix, cover the dish and cook for 10 minutes on MEDIUM, stirring occasionally. Add the red pepper and celery to the casserole and cook for a further 2 minutes on HIGH. Stir in the cashews, onions and bean sprouts. Serve with fried rice or crisp noodles. Best prepared for 2 people.

Turkey Korma (Mild Curry)

PREPARATION TIME: 15 minutes

MICROWAVE COOKING TIME:
10 minutes

SERVES: 1 person

1 turkey leg
2 tbsps chopped onion
1 tsp oil
1½ tsps butter or margarine
½ tbsp curry powder
1 tsp paprika
1 tsp ground coriander
1½ tbsps flour
½ cup chicken bouillon
1 tbsp golden raisins
1 tbsp roasted cashew nuts or shelled pistachio nuts
2 tsps unsweetened coconut
¼ cup plain yogurt
Salt and pepper

Skin and bone the turkey leg and cut the meat into 1" pieces. Use half and freeze the other half for use later. Heat the oil in a large casserole for 30 seconds on HIGH. Add the butter and, when melted, add the onion, turkey and spices. Cook for 3 minutes on HIGH to cook the spices. Add the flour and bouillon and stir to mix well. Cover the casserole and cook for 5 minutes on HIGH, stirring frequently until the turkey is tender. Add the raisins, coconut, nuts, salt, pepper and yogurt. Leave to stand, covered, for 1 minute. Serve with rice and chutney.
To serve 2 people, use the whole turkey leg and double all other ingredients. Cook the casserole for 8 minutes on HIGH.

Ham Steaks with Mango Sauce

PREPARATION TIME: 10 minutes

MICROWAVE COOKING TIME:
13 minutes

SERVES: 2 people

2 fully cooked ham slices (about ¼ lb each)
1 tbsp butter

SAUCE
1 ripe mango, peeled and thinly sliced
½ tsp ground ginger
Juice of half a lime
½ tsp soy sauce
Pinch Cayenne pepper
¼ tsp cornstarch
⅓ cup orange juice

Cut the ham slices around the outside at 2" intervals, ¼" in from the edge, to stop them from curling. Reserve 4 thin slices of mango and purée the rest in a food processor with the remaining sauce ingredients. Heat a browning dish on HIGH for 5 minutes. Put in the butter and the

Facing page: Fiery Duck (top) and Turkey Korma (Mild Curry) (bottom).

ham steaks and cook for 1 minute on HIGH. Turn the ham steaks once to brown both sides. Remove the ham from the dish to a casserole and pour over the puréed sauce ingredients. Cook, uncovered, for about 5 minutes on MEDIUM, or until the sauce has thickened. If necessary, remove the ham and keep warm while cooking the sauce for a further 2 minutes on HIGH. Garnish with the reserved mango slices. Serve with sesame stir-fry.

To serve one person, use 1 ham slice and ½ tbsp butter. Use full quantity sauce ingredients and cook for the same length of time as for 2 people.

Beef Roulades

PREPARATION TIME: 20 minutes

MICROWAVE COOKING TIME: 19 minutes

SERVES: 2 people

*4 pieces rump steak, cut thin and
    flattened
1 dill pickle, cut into quarters lengthwise
2 green onions, trimmed and cut in half
    lengthwise
1 tbsp oil*

SAUCE
*½ cup mushrooms, quartered
1½ tsp butter or margarine
2 tsps flour
¼ tsp thyme
1 bay leaf
⅔ cup beef bouillon
1 tbsp red wine
Salt and pepper
Gravy browning (if necessary)*

GARNISH
Buttered spinach pasta

Roll each of the beef slices around a quarter of the dill pickle and half a green onion. Sprinkle with pepper and fasten with wooden picks. Heat a browning dish on HIGH for 5 minutes. Put in the oil and add the roulades. Cook for 8 minutes, turning frequently. Remove from the dish and set aside in a casserole dish. Add the butter to the dish and allow to melt. Add the mushrooms and

cook for 1 minute on HIGH. Stir in the flour and cook for 2 minutes to brown lightly. Add the bouillon, wine, thyme and bay leaf, scraping any sediment off the surface of the browning dish. Add gravy browning for extra color if necessary. Season, and pour over the roulades. Cover the dish and cook for 12 minutes on MEDIUM. Test the meat with a knife and if not tender, cook for a further 3 minutes on HIGH. Serve with the pasta or French peas.

To serve one person, prepare only half the quantity of each ingredient and cook the roulades in the sauce for about 10 minutes on MEDIUM.

Alternatively, the full quantity recipe freezes well.

Mexican Pork Casserole

PREPARATION TIME: 15 minutes

MICROWAVE COOKING TIME: 28 minutes

SERVES: 2 people

*½ lb boneless pork loin, cut into 1" cubes
½ cup canned garbanzo beans/chickpeas
½ cup canned kidney beans
¼ cup chopped sweet red pepper*

¼ cup chopped green pepper
½ small chili pepper, finely chopped
¼ cup chopped onion
1 tbsp flour
2 tsps oil
¾ cup beef bouillon
1 tbsp instant coffee
½ clove garlic, crushed
¼ tsp ground cumin
¼ tsp ground coriander

GARNISH
Tortilla chips

Heat a browning dish for 5 minutes on HIGH. Put in the oil and add the pork cubes. Cook for 2 minutes on

Facing page: Veal Chops in Peppercorn Cream Sauce (top) and Ham Steaks with Mango Sauce (bottom). This page: Mexican Pork Casserole (top) and Beef Roulades (bottom).

HIGH, stirring frequently, until slightly browned. Add the cumin, coriander, garlic, onion and flour, and cook for 1-2 minutes on HIGH. Dissolve the instant coffee in the bouillon and add to the casserole, stirring well. Add the peppers, cover, and cook on MEDIUM for 17 minutes, or until the pork loses its pink color. Add the beans and heat

for 2 minutes on MEDIUM. Serve with tortilla chips if desired.
To serve 1 person, prepare full quantity casserole, and freeze half.

Veal Chops in Peppercorn Cream Sauce

PREPARATION TIME: 15 minutes

MICROWAVE COOKING TIME: 25 minutes

SERVES: 2 people

2 loin veal chops
1 tbsp butter or margarine
½ cup heavy cream
¼ cup chicken bouillon
2 tbsps brandy
1 tbsp green peppercorns, dried (or packed in brine, drained and rinsed)
½ cap pimento, diced
2 black olives, stoned and sliced thinly
Salt and pepper

Remove some of the fat from the outside of the chops. Heat a browning dish on HIGH for 5 minutes. Put in the butter or margarine and the chops. Cook for 3 minutes on HIGH, turning once, until both sides are lightly browned. Remove the chops to a casserole. De-glaze the dish with the bouillon and add the brandy, salt and pepper. Pour the sauce over the chops, cover with pierced plastic wrap, and cook on MEDIUM for 15 minutes or until the chops are tender. Add the peppercorns, pimento and olives during the last 3 minutes of cooking time. If the chops are not tender after 15 minutes, cook for an additional 2 minutes on MEDIUM. Add the cream and cook 1 minute on HIGH. Serve with zucchini rolls, leeks Provençale, or French peas.
To serve 1 person, cut the quantities of each ingredient by half and cook for the same length of time.

Microwave COOKING FOR 1&2

VEGETABLES

Corn on the Cob with Flavored Butters

PREPARATION TIME: 10 minutes

MICROWAVE COOKING TIME: 8 minutes

SERVES: 2 people

2 ears of corn
3 tbsps butter with a choice of:
½ tsp wholegrain mustard, or
½ tsp tomato paste and ¼ tsp basil, or
½ tsp garlic powder and ¼ tsp parsley, or
½ tsp chili powder

Clean the husks and silk from the ears of corn and wrap each in plastic wrap, or put into a roasting bag and seal tightly. Cook for about 8 minutes, turning once. Mix the butter with one or more of the flavoring choices and serve with the hot corn.

Leeks Provençale

PREPARATION TIME: 10 minutes

MICROWAVE COOKING TIME: 8 minutes

SERVES: 2 people

3 leeks, washed, trimmed and cut into
  2″ pieces
1 small clove garlic, finely chopped
2 tomatoes, chopped
1 tbsp oil
2 tbsps white wine
½ tsp thyme
1 tbsp chopped parsley
Salt and pepper

Put the oil into a 1 quart casserole,

and add the leeks and garlic, tossing to coat. Cook, uncovered, for 3 minutes on HIGH, stirring occasionally. Add the herbs, white wine, salt and pepper, and cover and

This page: Corn on the Cob with Flavored Butters. Facing page: French Peas (top) and Leeks Provençale (bottom).

51

cook for a further 5 minutes on HIGH. Add the tomatoes and cook for 1 minute on HIGH. Serve immediately.

To serve one person, use 1 large or 2 small leeks and half of each of the other ingredients. Cook the leeks for 2 minutes on HIGH and after adding the other ingredients, cook for a further 3-4 minutes on HIGH. Add the tomatoes and cook for 1 minute on HIGH.

Eggplant Niramish

PREPARATION TIME: 20 minutes

MICROWAVE COOKING TIME: 17 minutes

SERVES: 2 people

1 eggplant
2 tbsps butter
1 clove garlic, finely chopped
1 small onion, chopped
1 small potato, diced
1 small carrot, diced
¼ cup peas
1 cup canned tomatoes, chopped and juice reserved
1 tsp flour
¼ cup raisins
¼ cup pine nuts or chopped almonds
1 tbsp chopped coriander leaves or parsley
¼ tsp ground coriander
¼ tsp ground cumin
¼ tsp turmeric
¼ tsp fenugreek
¼ tsp ground ginger
Cayenne pepper
Paprika
Salt and pepper

GARNISH
¼ cup plain yogurt
Parsley or coriander leaves

Cut the eggplant in half lengthwise and score the flesh lightly. Sprinkle with salt and leave to stand for 20 minutes. The salt will draw out any bitterness. Rinse the eggplant well and pat dry. Melt the butter for 30 seconds on HIGH in a large casserole. Add the spices and cook for 2 minutes on HIGH. Add the onion, garlic, carrots and potatoes. Cover and cook for 3 minutes on

HIGH. Stir in the flour and add the tomato juice and pulp and chopped coriander or parsley. Cover the bowl and cook on HIGH for a further 5 minutes or until vegetables are just tender. Add the raisins, nuts and peas. Put the eggplant in another casserole, cover, and cook for 5 minutes on HIGH. Scoop out the flesh and reserve the skins. Mix the eggplant with the vegetable filling and fill the skins. Sprinkle with paprika and cook for 3 minutes on HIGH. Serve immediately. Top with a spoonful of yogurt and garnish with sprigs of parsley or coriander.

To serve 1 person, prepare the full quantity, serve one half and freeze the other.

French Peas

PREPARATION TIME: 10 minutes

MICROWAVE COOKING TIME: 6-10 minutes

SERVES: 2 people

1½ cups peas, fresh or frozen
4 leaves Romaine lettuce
½ cup parsley or chervil sprigs
½ cup small onions, peeled
1 tsp sugar
1 tbsp butter
1 tbsp flour
2 sticks celery, diced
½ cup chicken bouillon
Salt and pepper

If using fresh peas, shell them and combine with the celery, onions, half the bouillon, salt and pepper, and sugar in a 1 quart casserole. Cover and cook for 7 minutes on HIGH until almost tender. Add the lettuce and parsley (or chervil) and cook for a further 2 minutes on HIGH. Set aside. (If using frozen peas, combine the lettuce and parsley at the beginning and cook for a total of 5 minutes.) Melt the butter in a small bowl for 30 seconds on HIGH. Add the flour and remaining stock, and cook, uncovered, for 1 minute on HIGH. Stir into the peas, and serve. Best cooked for 2 people.

Stuffed Potatoes

PREPARATION TIME: 15 minutes

MICROWAVE COOKING TIME: 18 minutes, plus 5 minutes standing time

SERVES: 1 person

1 large baking potato
2 tsps chopped chives
2 tbsps milk
2 strips bacon
2 tbsps sour cream
1 tbsp crumbled blue cheese
1 tbsp shredded Cheddar cheese
1 tbsp dry seasoned breadcrumbs
Paprika
Salt and pepper

Heat a browning dish for 5 minutes on HIGH. Put in the bacon and cook for 2-3 minutes on HIGH, or until crisp. Crumble the bacon and set it aside. Pierce the potato skin several times with a fork. Put the potato on a plate and cook on HIGH for 5 minutes, or until soft. Turn over after 2 minutes. Cover it tightly in foil and leave it to stand for 5 minutes. Cut the potato in half lengthwise and scoop out the flesh, reserving the shells. Heat the milk for 30 seconds on HIGH, add to the potato with the sour cream and beat well. Add the chives, salt and pepper, bacon and blue cheese, and spoon into the potato shells. Sprinkle on the Cheddar cheese, crumbs and paprika. Cook on MEDIUM for 3 minutes and increase the setting to HIGH for 1 minute. Serve immediately.

For two people, use the full quantity recipe for a side dish, or double the quantity of each ingredient. Cook the potatoes for 7 minutes on HIGH, and the filled potato shells for 4 minutes on MEDIUM and 1 minute on HIGH.

Facing page: Eggplant Niramish (top) and Stuffed Potatoes (bottom).

Zucchini Rolls

PREPARATION TIME: 15 minutes

MICROWAVE COOKING TIME:
8 minutes

SERVES: 2 people

1 large zucchini
1 carrot, cut into 3" sticks
1 green pepper, cut into ½" slices
2 green onions, shredded lengthwise
Small bunch of whole fresh chives
¼ tsp herbs (thyme or basil)
1 tbsp butter
Juice of half a lemon
Salt and pepper

Trim the end of the zucchini and cut lengthwise into very thin slices. Spread evenly over the bottom of a large casserole. Pour on the lemon juice, cover, and cook for 1 minute to soften. Remove and set aside. In the same casserole, cook the carrot, covered, for 3 minutes on HIGH. Add the pepper and cook for a further 2 minutes on HIGH. Add the onion. Sprinkle with herbs and salt and pepper. Divide the vegetables evenly and place on top of the zucchini slices, twisting the ends of the zucchini around the piles of vegetables. Tie at both ends with the chives. Melt the butter in a small bowl for 30 seconds on HIGH. Pour the butter over the vegetables in the casserole, cover, and heat through for 1-2 minutes on HIGH before serving. Best cooked for 2 people.

Sesame Stir-fry

PREPARATION TIME: 15 minutes

MICROWAVE COOKING TIME:
7 minutes

SERVES: 2 people

2 tbsps oil
¼ lb pea pods
1 stick celery, sliced
2 ears baby corn, cut in half lengthwise
¼ cup water chestnuts, sliced
¼ cup mushrooms, sliced
1 cup bean sprouts
1 green onion, diagonally sliced
1 cup Chinese cabbage, shredded

½ tsp chopped ginger root
1 small sweet red pepper, thinly sliced
1 tbsp cornstarch
2 tbsps soy sauce
1 tbsp sherry
½ tsp sesame seed oil
1 tbsp sesame seeds
¼ cup water

Heat a browning tray for 5 minutes on HIGH. Put in 2 tbsps of oil and add all the vegetables except the Chinese cabbage and green onion. Toss in the oil and add the ginger and sesame seeds. Cook on HIGH for 4 minutes. Add the Chinese cabbage and bean sprouts and cook for 1 minute more on HIGH. Combine the cornstarch, sherry, soy sauce, water and sesame seed oil in a small

This page: Zucchini Rolls.
Facing page: Sesame Stir-fry.

bowl. Cook on HIGH for 2 minutes, or until clear. Pour over the vegetables and toss to coat before serving. To serve one person, cut the ingredient quantities by half and cook the vegetables for 3 minutes on HIGH. Add the cabbage and bean sprouts and cook for 30 seconds on HIGH. Cook the sauce ingredients for 2 minutes on HIGH.

Warm Vegetable Salad

PREPARATION TIME: 20 minutes

MICROWAVE COOKING TIME:
5 minutes

SERVES: 2 people

¼ cup shredded red cabbage
¼ cup green beans
¼ cup sliced mushrooms
4 green onions, trimmed
1 hard-boiled egg
Shredded lettuce

DRESSING
1½ tbsps oil
1 tbsp vinegar
1 tbsp Dijon mustard
½ tsp caraway seeds
Salt and pepper

Mix the dressing ingredients together
thoroughly. Chop the white of the egg
and push the yolk through a strainer.
Put the cabbage, beans, onions and
mushrooms into a 1 pint casserole
with 1 tbsp water and cook, covered,
for 5 minutes. Add the lettuce and
dressing during the last minute of
cooking, and toss well. Serve
garnished with the egg.
For one person, reduce the ingredient
quantities by half, except for the egg.
Cook the vegetables for 3-4 minutes
before adding the lettuce and
dressing.

Lima Beans, Carrots and Bacon with Mustard

PREPARATION TIME: 15 minutes

MICROWAVE COOKING TIME:
11 minutes

SERVES: 2 people

1 cup Lima beans
1 cup sliced carrots
2 strips bacon
1 tbsp Dijon mustard
1½ tbsps butter
Salt and pepper

Heat a browning dish for 5 minutes
on HIGH. Cook the bacon for
1-2 minutes on HIGH or until crisp.
Crumble the bacon and set it aside.

Put the beans into a 1 pint casserole
with 2 tbsps water and cook for 1
minute on HIGH. Peel off the outer
skin if desired and set the beans
aside. Put the carrots into the
casserole with 2 tbsps water. Cook,
uncovered, for 2 minutes on HIGH.
Add the peeled beans to the
casserole and cook for 1 minute more
on HIGH. Drain and keep warm.
Add the bacon to the beans and
carrots. In a small bowl, melt the
butter for 30 seconds on HIGH. Add

**This page: Warm Vegetable Salad
(top) and Lima Beans, Carrots and
Bacon with Mustard (bottom).
Facing page: Raspberry
Meringues.**

the salt and pepper, and beat in the
mustard until the sauce holds
together. Pour over the vegetables
and toss to serve.
For one person, cut the quantity of
each ingredient by half and cook for
half the stated time.

DESSERTS

Raspberry Meringues

PREPARATION TIME: 15 minutes

MICROWAVE COOKING TIME:
1 minutes

SERVES: 2 people

MERINGUES
1 egg white
1 cup powdered sugar
½ tsp raspberry flavoring
2 drops red food coloring

FILLING
½ cup cream, whipped
1 cup fresh or frozen raspberries
2 tbsps raspberry liqueur
Sugar

GARNISH
Powdered sugar
Cocoa

Put the egg white into a bowl and stir with a fork. Stir in the powdered sugar, adding enough to make a firm, pliable dough. Add the coloring and flavoring with the powdered sugar. Roll to ½" thick on a board sprinkled with powdered sugar. Cut into 2" heart shapes or rounds and place 4" apart on a microwave baking sheet lined with wax paper. If making heart shapes, have the points towards the middle. Cook for 1 minute on HIGH until firm and dry. Combine the raspberries, liqueur and sugar to taste. When the meringues are cool, fill with some of the raspberries and sandwich 2 of the meringues together with cream. Sprinkle the tops with powdered sugar and cocoa. Serve remaining raspberries separately.

thickened. Stir in the kirsch. Serve the pudding warm with the sauce, and whipped cream or ice cream if desired.

Oranges in Caramel Sauce

PREPARATION TIME: 15 minutes

MICROWAVE COOKING TIME: 4 minutes

SERVES: 1 person

1 orange
3 tbsps brown sugar
¼ cup water
1 tsp Grand Marnier
½ tsp cornstarch
¼ tsp lemon juice

Peel the orange, removing all the white pith. Set aside the whole orange and scrape all the pith off the peel. Cut the orange peel into thin strips. Mix the brown sugar, water and lemon juice and heat for 2 minutes on HIGH. Stir occasionally to help dissolve the sugar. Mix the cornstarch and the liqueur and stir into the sugar syrup. Cook for 1 minute on HIGH to thicken. Add the orange peel to the hot sauce and pour over the orange. Heat through for 1 minute on HIGH, turning once. Serve immediately.

Cherry and Almond Bread Pudding

PREPARATION TIME: 15 minutes

MICROWAVE COOKING TIME: 9-14 minutes

SERVES: 2 people

¼ cup chopped, unblanched almonds
1 egg
¾ cup light cream
1½ cups brioche, cut into 2" cubes
¼ tsp cinnamon
3 tbsps sugar
½ cup pitted dark, sweet cherries, canned, and juice reserved

SAUCE
½ cup reserved cherry juice
¼ tsp cornstarch
1 tbsp cherry brandy or kirsch
¼ tsp almond extract

Heat a browning dish for 5 minutes on HIGH. Put in the almonds and cook on HIGH for about 3 minutes, stirring every 30 seconds until golden brown. Combine the egg and cream. Beat in the sugar and cinnamon, and stir in the bread cubes and cherries. Pour into a 1 pint casserole and cook for 5-10 minutes on HIGH, or until the center is just set. Leave to stand for 2 minutes before serving. Combine the juice, extract and cornstarch. Cook on HIGH for 1 minute, stirring once or twice until

Cranberry Crisp

PREPARATION TIME: 10 minutes

MICROWAVE COOKING TIME: 11-12 minutes

SERVES: 2 people

FILLING
½ cup orange juice or cranberry juice
1 cup fresh cranberries
2 tsps sugar
2 tsps cornstarch
¼ tsp cinnamon

This page: Oranges in Caramel Sauce. Facing page: Cherry and Almond Bread Pudding (top) and Cranberry Crisp (bottom).

TOPPING

¾ cup crunchy oatmeal cereal
2 tbsps butter or margarine
1 tbsp flour
2 tbsps honey

Combine the filling ingredients in a small casserole or individual dishes and cook on HIGH for 3-4 minutes, or until the mixture thickens. Stir twice during cooking and set aside. Toss the flour and cereal together. Melt the butter and mix in. Sprinkle over the top of the cranberry filling and cook for 4 minutes on HIGH. Drizzle over the honey and cook for a further 4 minutes on HIGH. Serve warm, with whipped cream.

Black Velvet and White Lace

PREPARATION TIME: 25 minutes

MICROWAVE COOKING TIME:
5 minutes

SERVES: 2 people

BLACK VELVET

½ cup unsalted butter
¼ cup sugar
2 eggs, separated
4 squares cooking chocolate
1 tbsp instant coffee, dissolved in 2 tbsps
*   boiling water*

WHITE LACE

¼ lb white chocolate

Soften the butter in a medium-sized bowl for 20 seconds on HIGH. Add sugar and beat until light and fluffy. Add the egg yolks one at a time, beating between each addition until the mixture is light and lemon-colored. Melt the chocolate with the strong coffee mixture for 2 minutes on MEDIUM. Whisk the egg whites until stiff but not dry. Beat the warm chocolate into the egg yolks quickly and heat 2 minutes on MEDIUM, stirring every 30 seconds. Fold in the egg whites. Refrigerate until firm. Put the white chocolate into a small bowl and melt on MEDIUM for 1-2 minutes, stirring once. Fill a small pastry bag fitted with a writing tube. Pipe out a lacy pattern onto wax

paper and refrigerate to harden. To serve, scoop out spoonfuls of the mousse into bowls or onto plates. Pour over 1 tbsp of coffee liqueur if desired. Carefully peel off the white chocolate lace patterns and use to decorate the black velvet mousse.

Brown Sugar Bananas

PREPARATION TIME: 10 minutes

MICROWAVE COOKING TIME:
3½ minutes

SERVES: 2 people

2 bananas
2 tbsps butter or margarine
4 tbsps brown sugar
Grated rind and juice of 1 lemon
¼ cup whole pecans
2 tbsps dark rum

Peel the bananas and cut in half lengthwise. Brush all surfaces with lemon juice to prevent browning. Melt the butter in a baking dish for 30 seconds on HIGH. Add the lemon juice and rind. Add the bananas and cook on MEDIUM for 2 minutes until heated through. Remove the bananas and keep them warm. Stir in the sugar and cook for 1 minute on HIGH, stirring frequently until bubbling. Add the pecans and rum, and pour over the bananas to serve.

Orange Creams

PREPARATION TIME: 15-20 minutes

MICROWAVE COOKING TIME:
5 minutes

SERVES: 2 people

2 tbsps orange juice
¾ cup milk
2 eggs, beaten
¼ cup sugar
Ground ginger
1 tangerine
1 egg white
Granulated sugar

Peel the tangerine, removing all the white pith. Leave the membranes around each segment. Beat the egg white lightly and dip in the segments. Roll in the granulated sugar and put on wax paper to set. Heat the milk on HIGH for 2 minutes in a 2 cup measure: do not allow the milk to boil. Add the orange juice. Mix the eggs, sugar, ginger and a pinch of salt. Beat well and gradually add the milk. Pour into 2 custard cups, and put them into a baking dish with hot water to come ¼" up the outsides of the cups. Cover the baking dish loosely with plastic wrap and cook for 3 minutes on LOW. If softly set, remove from the oven and allow to cool. If still liquid, cook for 1½ minutes more on LOW, watching carefully. Serve warm or cold with the frosted tangerines.

Grenadine and Lemon Pears

PREPARATION TIME: 15 minutes

MICROWAVE COOKING TIME:
15-20 minutes

SERVES: 2 people

2 fresh pears, approximately equal size
Juice and peel of 1 lemon
1 cup Grenadine syrup
½ cup light corn syrup
¼ cup water

GARNISH

Mint leaves

Mix the corn syrup, water and Grenadine syrup and cook for 5 minutes on HIGH. Peel the lemon and cut the peel into very thin strips. Squeeze the juice from the lemon and mix with the syrup. Peel the pears and leave whole. Leave the stem attached, but remove the eye on

Facing page: Orange Creams (top) and Brown Sugar Bananas (bottom).

the base. Put the pears into a small, deep bowl, big enough for them to stand upright in. Pour over the syrup and cover the bowl with pierced plastic wrap. Cook for 5 minutes on HIGH. Lower the setting to MEDIUM and cook 5 minutes, or until tender. If not tender after 5

minutes, cook for a further 5 minutes on MEDIUM. Remove the pears from the syrup and re-boil the syrup for 5 minutes on HIGH to reduce. Stir in the peel and coat over the pears. Garnish with the mint leaves, and serve hot or cold with whipped cream.

This page: Black Velvet and White Lace. Facing page: Grenadine and Lemon Pears.

INDEX